T0208350

Encounters with Jesus by the Water

Candy Porostosky

WESTBOW
PRESS®
A DIVISION OF THOMAS NELSON
& ZONDERVAN

Copyright © 2019 Candy Porostosky.

All rights reserved. No part of this book may be used or reproduced by any means, graphic, electronic, or mechanical, including photocopying, recording, taping or by any information storage retrieval system without the written permission of the author except in the case of brief quotations embodied in critical articles and reviews.

This book is a work of non-fiction. Unless otherwise noted, the author and the publisher make no explicit guarantees as to the accuracy of the information contained in this book and in some cases, names of people and places have been altered to protect their privacy.

WestBow Press books may be ordered through booksellers or by contacting:

WestBow Press
A Division of Thomas Nelson & Zondervan
1663 Liberty Drive
Bloomington, IN 47403
www.westbowpress.com
1 (866) 928-1240

Because of the dynamic nature of the Internet, any web addresses or links contained in this book may have changed since publication and may no longer be valid. The views expressed in this work are solely those of the author and do not necessarily reflect the views of the publisher, and the publisher hereby disclaims any responsibility for them.

Any people depicted in stock imagery provided by Getty Images are models, and such images are being used for illustrative purposes only. Certain stock imagery © Getty Images.

Scripture quotations marked (NIV) are taken from the Holy Bible, New International Version®, NIV®. Copyright © 1973, 1978, 1984, 2011 by Biblica, Inc.™ Used by permission of Zondervan. All rights reserved worldwide. www.zondervan.com The "NIV" and "New International Version" are trademarks registered in the United States Patent and Trademark Office by Biblica, Inc.™

ISBN: 978-1-9736-7031-5 (sc)
ISBN: 978-1-9736-7030-8 (hc)
ISBN: 978-1-9736-7032-2 (e)

Library of Congress Control Number: 2019910727

Print information available on the last page.

WestBow Press rev. date: 8/21/2019

Acknowledgments

Special thanks to my husband Mark, who from the very beginning has been very supportive of this writing endeavor, reading draft after draft after draft, and keeping the house in order while I zoned out and stared endlessly into a computer screen, typing out the thoughts God had put in my heart. I could not have completed this project without your help. You are a blessing to me!

Thanks to my children, Monica and Mark, who listened to me ramble on and on about this project. Your love and encouragement mean so much to me.

To the ladies of the initial study by the lake: I cannot thank you enough for the time we spent together studying the Word of God together on the beach with pen and Bible in hand. You were my inspiration and joy throughout this journey.

Thanks for my sister Rebecca for making several trips to the beach to find the perfect sunset for the cover of the book.

Thanks to Susan for taking the time in a busy senior year of college to use her artistic skills to create simple, but interesting graphics that captured the story of each lesson throughout the book.

I am so thankful to Westbow Press for all of their encouragement and help along the way. What a joy it is to call and have a happy voice on the other end answering my unending questions. I am sure our journey is only just begun. It has been my pleasure to work with you.

Thanks to Charlie, my dog, who sat by me on the couch,

wondering why I was paying more attention my laptop than him. ☺

Last, but not least, I am forever thankful for what Jesus, my Lord and Savior, has done in my life. I give Him all the glory for anything good that is accomplished from someone reading this book. May Jesus be as real to you as He has been to me.

Foreword

In the summer of 2018, after leading a ladies' Bible study on the beach of Lake Erie, the idea of this book was born. We met by the lake to put ourselves in a similar setting to the one Jesus was in when he was baptized, called the disciples into full-time ministry, taught in parables, walked on water, and fixed breakfast for Peter and several other disciples shortly after His resurrection. With the sound of seagulls flying overhead and the water splashing ashore, we looked at the story of the woman at the well. All of us were in different stages in our walks with Christ, but we all learned things that could be applied to our lives to encourage us and help us grow in faith. Also, the fellowship was sweet!

With the sound of summer rain all around us, we enjoyed an intimate time of studying under a pavilion. We meditated about God's love for us and the world we live in, shared our concerns, and prayed for each other. For me, the benefits of the study seemed to be too good to not share with anyone who was willing to read it.

Whether sitting by a body of water or in the quiet of your home, whether on vacation or engulfed in daily living, the insights from each lesson can be refreshing and enlightening. Each lesson can be studied as a whole or broken into parts, and each section ends with a time of reflection as you think about what the Holy Spirit is saying to you. Whether you have chosen this resource to use as a Bible study or as a devotional, I am thankful you have decided to join me on the journey to *Encounters with Jesus by the Water*.

—Candy Porostosky

Contents

LESSON 1
The Baptism of Jesus
Scripture References: Luke 1:5–17;
Matthew 3; John 1:19–34; Matthew 11:1–19

In reading through the four Gospels—Matthew, Mark, Luke, and John—the first encounter regarding Jesus being near water is His baptism by John the Baptist. To appreciate the baptism of Jesus, one must have some knowledge regarding the life and history of John and the role he played in the beginnings of Jesus's ministry and life on earth.

John the Baptist's Parents and His Purpose
Luke 1:13–17

In looking at the life of John, there is no doubt he was clearly destined to be the forerunner of Christ. His miraculous birth to Zechariah and Elizabeth, who were much older than most parents, came with a clear and divine calling. The announcement of his birth, received from an angel, came with instructions and purpose. John would make people ready for the Messiah.

The responsibility of John's parents came not only from the angel regarding the birth of their son but also from the Old Testament prophecies that would be fulfilled through his birth. Isaiah 40:3 (NIV) is one of those verses, and Malachi 3:1 (NIV) is another.

> A voice of one calling: "In the wilderness prepare the way for the LORD; make straight in the desert a highway for our God." (Isaiah 40:3 NIV)

> "I will send my messenger, who will prepare the way before me. Then suddenly the Lord you are seeking will come to his temple; the messenger of the covenant, whom you desire, will come," says the LORD Almighty. (Malachi 3:1 NIV)

During the time period in which John was born, history tells us there was much political unrest, religious hypocrisy, and a period of silence that lasted about four hundred years. The Old Testament scriptures prior to this time period display the Israelites' ongoing disobedience. Because of this disobedience, they were without a voice from God and lived under the rule of the Roman Empire with no prophet or king. There was no trust in the government and no prophet to give them hope or prod them toward right living. They were living with memories of what God had done for their ancestors and hoping the promised Messiah would come someday.

Like Zechariah and Elizabeth, parents often struggle bringing up children in our world. The responsibility of raising them to be godly in an ungodly world and helping them discover and develop their God-given purpose can weigh heavily on their hearts. Sleepless nights and prayers of intercession that God will help them make the right choices at every stage of life are common for godly parents.

A senior pastor who mentored my husband and me in our young adult years often said, "When children are young, they step on your toes; when they are older, they step on your heart."

As children approach their teen years and move into adulthood, a parent's concerns change from worrying about the child falling down the stairs and breaking a bone to worrying about how the life choices they make will affect the rest of their lives. It was no different for Elizabeth and Zechariah. They were "righteous before God, walking in all the commandments and ordinances of the Lord blamelessly" (Luke 1:6). As godly parents, the fact that God called on John to "make ready a people prepared for the Lord" had to have kept them up at night wondering how this prophecy would unfold. They were no different from us and how we are concerned about our children's futures.

Zechariah and Elizabeth's righteous lifestyle leaves us to wonder the affect this would have on their parenting of John. We know how important the holy life they lived was to John's life because of how much the scripture emphasizes it. John's parents were not wishy-washy in their faith. They were godly examples to John. They not only talked about God; they lived His Word. They did not say one thing and do another. Since ideas are more caught than taught, it is important that our children see us, in everyday life, living for Jesus, not just with our words but also in our actions.

As a child of a home mission pastor, the church was definitely a big part of my life. What I value and remember most were the

Bible teachings of my father and how those teachings were actively carried out in his daily life. Living as an example in all the disciplines of God's Word is more valuable than simply talking about them and going to church once a week. The way we, as parents, live during our children's formative years leaves lasting impressions on the rest of their life and influences their adult decisions.

For the parents whose hearts are breaking because, though they have lived faithfully for Jesus and raised their children to the best of their abilities, they are now observing their children walking away from the faith: I encourage you to keep loving and praying for your children. As a child moves into young adulthood, with all the influences of college and the workplace, they may begin to question their upbringing. Though it breaks our hearts to see them floundering in their faith, at some point, we have to let go and put them into God's hands, praying and trusting God to care for them as He has cared for us. Never stop praying. Never stop believing they will return to Jesus. Trust in God. He has a plan for their lives—even when you cannot see it. Restore your hope as you think about young couples who have walked away from God but are now faithfully serving God as a family. As a parent, however, it is hard to watch this unfold. When we dedicated ourselves to raising our children to serve the Lord, we knew God had put them into our lives for a time—and at some point, we would need to trust God enough to complete the work.

For parents who came to know Jesus later in life and still bear regrets and forbidding memories of how they lived their lives in front of their children and spouses, remember that God forgives. Over the years, I have heard many stories of parents going back to their children and asking for forgiveness. The acceptance of a changed life and actions may not come instantaneously. Trust is not easily regained. Keep living faithfully for Jesus in front of your children. A true rebirth because of God is hard to ignore. No matter the outcome, continue to pray for your children and show them Jesus's love through your interactions with them. When they seem to look at you with reservation, don't get defensive and try to force your new beliefs on them. On the other hand, don't run away or withdraw. Instead, be the parent you wish you would have always been. Accept the grace and mercy God has given you and extend the same to your children. Season any truth you speak with the love that comes from God deep inside you. In whatever situation you currently are facing, work towards maintaining healthy boundaries and relationships with your adult children. Try not to internalize any of their hurtful remarks. Don't ever give up praying for them. Enlist the prayers and godly advice of a few close friends to help you get through difficult times.

Whether children continue in the faith or wander, parenting never ends. With adult children, it is hard to know when to speak up or bite our tongues, but they will always need our love, our prayers, and our examples. When you have done your best, hold fast to Proverbs 22:6 (NIV): "Start children off on the way they should go, and even when they are old they will not turn from it."

As a parent, my children mean the world to me. What I pray for them more than anything is that they have thriving relationships with Jesus Christ that carry them through this life and to eternity. As their personal Zechariah and Elizabeth, I consider it an honor and a responsibility to parent them and show them Jesus in every stage of their lives.

Reflection: Who is your Zechariah and Elizabeth? Who are you Zechariah and Elizabeth to? What changes do you need to make in order to be a better example for the young lives you lead or parent?

John the Baptist's Lifestyle
Matthew 3:4–6

As an adult, John was unique. His fashion statements and culinary delights made quite an impression. In Matthew 3:4, we read that his clothing was made of camel's hair, and he wore a leather belt around his waist. His food choice was locusts and wild honey. He also refrained from alcohol (Luke 1:15). Unlike the religious sects of the day, he was less than charismatic and impressive in appearance and lifestyle, but he had a message from God—and people who were seeking truth were strangely drawn to him.

Often, we put an emphasis on the visual instead of what we cannot see. We are easily impressed by a person's appearance, age, attention to fashion, title, abilities, talents, personableness, achievements, and wealth. Though we may be easily sidetracked by pomp and circumstance, God is not. Success in God's eyes does not depend so much on the outward as on the inward.

We are reminded of this in 1 Samuel 16. Samuel was looking for a king to replace King Saul. Under God's direction, Samuel went to the house of Jesse to find the next king. As each one of Jesse's sons came before him, they all had qualities that were appealing. God kept saying, "This is not the one."

> But the LORD said to Samuel, "Do not consider his appearance or his height, for I have rejected him. The LORD does not look at the things people look at. People look at the outward appearance, but the LORD looks at the heart." (1 Samuel 16:7 NIV)

God's most unlikely choice was David, the least favorite in the family. John was definitely God's choice as well. Despite John being in the desert and his appearance and fire-and-brimstone preaching, people came from all over to hear his message, confess their sins, and be baptized.

Be yourself. Whatever God has called you to do, do it. God will take care of the rest. Current wealth, location, and appearance have little to do with it. Stop using these things as excuses to not do what God has put in your heart to do. God is not limited by our present situations. David, the psalmist, was not the people's first choice, but God made it clear to Samuel that outward appearances had little to do with an individual's usefulness. Instead, it is the condition of the heart that matters. Use the current means that God has given you for His glory. Have a heart after God, like David did. In His timing and His way, He will direct and make a way to bring about the purpose He has for you.

Despite the things we think we lack, God can use us. Most of the things we think are impressive are not impressive to God. He looks for pure motives, a holy life, and a heart that loves and sees Him as more valuable than all else. God looks for someone who is faithful, available, and willing to learn and grow in faith. He looks for those who are more concerned about pleasing God than pleasing people. When our weaknesses, shortcomings, lack of confidence, lack of resources, and fears cause us to lean on Jesus, He uses us in spite of ourselves. In the end, He gets the recognition instead of us. Despite John's obvious idiosyncrasies, he was a history maker for God because of his zeal and obedience.

✎ *Refection: Have you ever been persuaded by a person's abilities. looks. or personality only to be disappointed later because of their lack of character or motives? What is holding you back from believing God can use you. accepting that God can use you. or allowing God to use you?*

Riverside Ministry
Matthew 3:1–2

John's ministry and message was that of repentance. *Merriam-Webster* gives the definition for the word *repent* as "to turn from sin and dedicate oneself to the amendment of one's life."[1] In other words, there is an about-face regarding the way someone has been living and behaving. A change in action also becomes apparent. True repentance is different from being caught because the person is sincerely sorry. The words of a person who pleads for forgiveness by proclaiming remorse for his or her actions are empty unless there is a transformation in their conduct.

From the beginning of our faith journey and throughout our walk with God, there will be times when God will call us to repent. Romans 3:23 says, "All have sinned and come short of the glory of God." Acknowledging sin in our lives is the first step to following Jesus. We have to realize that we are not—and cannot be—righteous on our own. Without the realization that we are sinners and need to repent and ask forgiveness for our sins, we cannot take the next step of truly following Jesus.

Repentance, however, is not a onetime occurrence. As we walk with God, He often reveals sin in our lives for which we need to ask forgiveness. Responding to that nudge of the Holy Spirit, relinquishing our pride, and realizing we are not good enough on our own is a prerequisite for experiencing forgiveness. Being truly sorry enough to ask Jesus to forgive us and fill us with His Holy Spirit to overcome sin in our lives is a sign of a repentant heart, a heart that wants to do what is right. The message of repentance that John preached is as relative today as it was then. A pure heart

---

[1] *Merriam-Webster*, s.v. "repent (*v.*)," https://www.merriam-webster.com/dictionary/repent.

without the bondage of unrepentant sin experiences the blessings of God and the promise of eternal life.

🖎 *Reflection: Think about a time when God convicted you of sin, causing you to repent. How did you feel? What was the end result?*

Riverside Confrontation
Matthew 3:7–12

Even the religious leaders of the day—the Pharisees and Saducees—came to hear John speak. He spoke to them directly and without reserve. He was not afraid of speaking the truth. Being spoken to with such direct authority, being called a "brood of vipers," and hearing John's declaration of judgment on them if they did not repent could not have been easy.

To understand why he was so direct, one would have to know more about the Pharisees and the Saducees. In researching the difference between Pharisees and Saducees, I found the following information on www.gotquestions.com. "Both Pharisees and Saducees were religious sects within Judaism during the time of Christ, both honored Moses and the Law, and both had a measure of political power."[2] However, there are differences between them. The following quote from www.gotquestions.com explains these differences.

> The differences between the Pharisees and the Sadducees are known to us through a couple of passages of Scripture and through the extant writings of the Pharisees. Religiously, the Sadducees were more conservative in one doctrinal area: they insisted on a literal interpretation of the text of Scripture; the Pharisees, on the other hand, gave oral tradition equal authority to the written Word of God. If the Sadducees couldn't find a command in the Tanakh, they dismissed it as manmade.
>
> Given the Pharisees' and the Sadducees' differing views of Scripture, it's no surprise that they argued over certain doctrines. The Sadducees

---

[2] "What are the differences between the Sadducees and Pharisees?" Got Questions, https://www.gotquestions.org/Sadducees-Pharisees.html.

rejected a belief in the resurrection of the dead (Matthew 22:23; Mark 12:18–27; Acts 23:8), but the Pharisees did believe in the resurrection. The Sadducees denied the afterlife, holding that the soul perished at death, but the Pharisees believed in an afterlife and in an appropriate reward and punishment for individuals. The Sadducees rejected the idea of an unseen, spiritual world, but the Pharisees taught the existence of angels and demons in a spiritual realm.

John was confronting their emphasis on man-made rules, superiority, self-righteousness, and judgmental religiosity against everyone else over having hearts that were pure. When it came to what they believed, they dotted their I's and crossed their T's. Their rituals and outward appearances gave them the appearance of being spiritual, but their hearts were far from God. Their religious pride kept them from abandoning their own self-righteousness and acknowledging their need for repentance.

As a worship leader, I am very sensitive to these next verses, which speak to religious activities that are done out of tradition. It is easy to speak about everyone else's religious rituals and be blinded to the reality that we often have our own. When you do something for long enough, like leading worship, it is easy to do the same things over and over. From all outside appearances, it looks like authentic worship. As you read the following verses, let God show you how, like the Pharisees and Sadducees, you may have allowed religious activities to take the place of the spiritual relationship God wants to have with you.

> Away with the noise of your songs! I will not listen to the music of your harps. But let justice roll on like a river, righteousness like a never-failing stream! (Amos 5:23–24 NIV)

For I desire mercy, not sacrifice, and acknowledgment of God rather than burnt offerings. (Hosea 6:6 NIV)

"The multitude of your sacrifices—what are they to me?" says the LORD. "I have more than enough of burnt offerings, of rams and the fat of fattened animals; I have no pleasure in the blood of bulls and lambs and goats. When you come to appear before me, who has asked this of you, this trampling of my courts?

Stop bringing meaningless offerings! Your incense is detestable to me. New Moons, Sabbaths, and convocations—I cannot bear your worthless assemblies. Your New Moon feasts and your appointed festivals I hate with all my being. They have become a burden to me; I am weary of bearing them. When you spread out your hands in prayer, I hide my eyes from you; even when you offer many prayers, I am not listening. Your hands are full of blood!

Wash and make yourselves clean. Take your evil deeds out of my sight; stop doing wrong. Learn to do right; seek justice. Defend the oppressed. Take up the cause of the fatherless; plead the case of the widow. (Isaiah 1:11–17 NIV)

In Isaiah 1:16–17, God is clear, and He does not leave us wondering what He desires. God constantly reminds me that—more than anything else—he wants me to spend time with Him in prayer and in His Word. Busy activities, whether religious in nature or personal hobbies, rob me of my time with Him and can take me away from putting Him first. He wants me to operate from a clean heart, which means truly living what I sing and preach.

🖎 *Reflection: While we don't offer animal sacrifices, what types of rituals and practices do we do out of habit? What kinds of things do we do in front of people but neglect to do when we are in private? What do we do because people are watching or do out of obligation instead of from our hearts?*

Riverside Jealousy
John 1:19–28

John's message clearly indicated the need for repentance, foretold the kingdom of heaven coming through salvation in Jesus, and implied judgment for those who do not repent. In John 1:19–28, the Jewish leaders were coming to see John, but this message of repentance was not the message they came to hear. This passage revealed their true motives: they were concerned about who he was and the amount of influence he had. They were not interested in repentance or being baptized by him. Their hearts were cold as ice when it came to receiving the message John preached. They were looking for something that would discredit him and a reason people should not follow him.

Seemingly, the Pharisees and Sadducees were jealous of John's followers and popularity, but John made it clear to them that he was not Elijah. He denied any connection to being the Messiah—but only to prepare people to receive the coming Messiah (Luke 1:16–17). He was clear to point people toward the One who was to come. In John 3:30, John, speaking of Jesus, said, "He must increase, but I must decrease."

Beware of spiritual leaders who have a tendency to become heroes or who seem to draw more attention to themselves than to Jesus Christ. This is a sober reminder that whatever God has called us to do is not a competition or a popularity contest. If we feel a twinge of envy or a temptation to please others more than God, we need to repent and return to our first love. We are not supposed to create a following of ourselves; we are supposed to point people toward the Savior of the world, Jesus.

🖎 *Reflection: Can you think of any examples of when someone seemed to draw more attention to themselves than to Jesus? Have you ever been tempted to do so? Do you ever feel like you don't get credit for what you do for Him and wish someone would notice?*

Riverside Revelations
Matthew 3:13–17; John 1:29–34

John was preaching and baptizing when Jesus arrived on the scene. That was the moment John was waiting for: the fulfillment of his calling, when he would reveal who the Messiah was.

Can you imagine being there that day as Jesus came to John to be baptized? I am sure my response would be the same as John's: "I need to be baptized by you—not the other way around!"

In the Gospel of John's account of this interaction, John identified Jesus as the "Lamb of God." To the Jews, the Passover lamb had much significance, and labeling Jesus as the "Lamb" had spiritual implications to John's disciples. However, to the unbelieving Jewish religious leaders, it was heresy.

History tells us of the exodus of God's chosen people out of Egypt. Moses gave specific instructions the night before their escape from slavery and their exit toward the Promised Land. The most significant instruction was to sacrifice a lamb without spot or blemish and to paint the doorposts with its blood. The death angel would pass over any house with that blood on its doorpost. For those that did not, the firstborn son of the household would die. Of course, before sunrise, Pharaoh granted the Israelites permission to leave (Exodus 12).

In light of this story, we can understand how the phrase "the Lamb of God" had more implications than were stated in the scripture. It spoke of the death that was to come when Jesus was "led like a lamb to the slaughter" and was crucified (Isaiah 53:7). It declared His very reason for existence: "to take away the sin of the world." It revealed that He was God since no one could take away sins but God.

The statement also exposed His sinlessness. When John announced Jesus as the Lamb of God, he was proclaiming that this "Lamb" was without spot or blemish, which also could have been a reason for his hesitancy in baptizing Him. Up to that point, everyone he had baptized was being baptized because of their confession of sins. Jesus, without sin, was baptized as our example. When we commemorate the Lord's Supper or celebrate Easter, we are remembering the time when Jesus, the sinless God-man—fully God, fully man—became our sacrificial Lamb on the cross to forgive us of all our sins.

In John 1:30, even though Jesus was chronologically born after John, John announced Him as being "before him," which ultimately proclaimed Him to have been before time, God in the flesh, the Messiah.

Last, but not least, God in His great wisdom, gave John the Baptist confirmation that Jesus was the Messiah by using visual and auditory signs. He was the One who would come to save people from their sins.

🖎 *Reflection: Spend some time remembering when the Holy Spirit revealed to you that Jesus was the Lamb of God. If you are with others. share your personal testimony. Then. end with a time of giving thanks for knowing Jesus. the Lamb of God.*

Riverside Doubts
Matthew 11:1–19

While John the Baptist was in prison, his memories of the events that occurred by the Jordan River began to fade. He was imprisoned for speaking the truth to Herod about marrying his brother's wife. John the Baptist even began to question what he had proclaimed as truth at Jesus's baptism. In Matthew 11, he sent the other disciples on a mission to find out if Jesus was in fact the Messiah.

It is easy to believe when everything is going as planned and we are at the peak of our revelation of God. When we find ourselves in the "dungeon of a prison," we begin to waver about God's goodness. Jesus in His gracious way answered John's inquiry and sent John's disciples on their way, satisfied with the information they had seen and heard. It is a lesson to us all to reach up when we find ourselves in this situation and seek out the truth. It is easy to find someone to gripe with and wallow in our own self-pity and doubt, but when we reach up, God reaches down and confirms His love for us. He enriches our faith and endows in us the strength to carry on to the end. I love that Jesus did not scold him for his doubt. I love that Jesus answered his questions. He cared about John deeply—just as He cares for us.

🕮 Reflection: Can you remember a time when you began to doubt? How did God confirm your faith? Can you remember a time when you needed to remind yourself of past answers to prayer and how God brought you through a difficult time to build your faith that He would do it again?

Like John, despite the current political climate and culture, we need to point others to Jesus. The message is simple. It starts with repentance and living a life that is different from the norm. The motives in our hearts must be pure. Despite times of uneasy confrontations, jealousy, and misjudgments, the revelation of who Jesus is carries us through. No matter what season of life we find ourselves in, Jesus is still the Lamb of God who takes away the sins of the world!

LESSON 2
The Calling of Disciples
Scripture References: John 1:35–49; Luke 5:1–11

Lesson 1 was about Jesus's baptism, and the study was dedicated to learning about the life of John and how he played an important role in preparing the way for Jesus to come on the scene.

John clearly did this as he preached, taught his followers about the fallacies of the religious leaders of the day, and baptized them for the remission of their sins. His message was about turning to God and away from sin and the religiosity of the day and preparing for who was to come.

While the calling of the disciples can be confusing, in reading all accounts from the four Gospels, we see that there are at least two disciples who knew Jesus before He called them from their fishing boats to be his full-time disciples. They knew Him because of John the Baptist.

From the seaside experiences we will study, we will learn about their responses, their relationships, and their eagerness to share. We will also see how being in the presence of Jesus convicted and changed them, the miracle that sealed their belief in Jesus as the Messiah, and the sacrifices they were willing to make because of Him.

Seaside Response
John 1:35–40

They had been followers of John, but once they met Jesus, their immediate response was to figure out where He was staying and spend the day with Him. I have to ask myself, "When was the last time I set aside an entire day to spend with Jesus?" A day to meditate on God's Word, listen to worship music and to pray. Parts of days for sure—but all day? Even the Sabbath, which is a day to observe and keep holy, gets convoluted with activities that take away from its purpose of being the Lord's day. Why is it that we can so easily obey the other nine commandments, but the fourth commandment, which asks us to observe the Sabbath (Exodus 20), we seem to obey only when it is convenient?

With the increase of yoga and Eastern medicine practices, which encourage meditation as part of a daily routine, people of all walks of life seem to be more aware of the need to shut down. As Christians, we need to be aware that God set it up long ago that we take the time to "be still" and meditate on His Word each day (Psalm 46:10). Daniel prayed three times a day (Daniel 6:10). David gave praise to God seven times a day (Psalm 119:164).

There is nothing more refreshing than setting aside time by yourself to get away from it all, to read God's Word, and to spend some uninterrupted time of prayer where God Himself can speak into our lives. Just as a married couple needs to set aside undistracted time for each other—away from the demands of family, work, and ministry—we need to set aside time to be with the love of our life, Jesus Christ. Turn off the cell phones, put aside the electronic devices, and spend quality time with the One who cares the most about us.

Perhaps it was the mentoring of John that caused the disciples to hunger for truth. Whatever the case, their desire to spend the day with Jesus is certainly an example to us. Since time quickly gets away from us, and the demands of life squelch what matters most, taking the time to be with Jesus and learning from Him may seem impossible. Taking baby steps may include setting the alarm fifteen minutes early to pray and read a scripture. Then, if the schedule allows, put a date on the calendar for a day with Jesus, attend a Bible study, or sign up for a conference. For smartphone users, Bible apps make it possible to have scriptures pop up during the day to give that moment with the Lord. These are just a few ideas to help keep you centered and grounded in Christ. Ask God to help you set aside alone time with Him, so like the disciples, you will draw near to God, be engulfed in His presence, glean everything you can, and continue to grow in His Word.

✎ *Reflection: What changes do you sense that the Holy Spirit is impressing upon you to make so that you have time with Jesus?*

Seaside Sharing
John 1:41–19

After spending the day with Jesus, the first thing Andrew did was share the good news with his brother, Simon, and introduce him to Jesus. We also read about what Philip told Nathanael. From the very start of their relationship with Jesus, they were compelled to tell others about Him. They started with those who were closest in relationship to them.

Though it seems to be a very simple point, and one that should be very apparent to us, before anyone can come to follow Jesus, someone has to open their mouth so the good news of the Savior can be heard (Romans 10:14–15). It pains me to realize how often I get tongue-tied when talking to an unbeliever about Christ. Because of my faith and love for Him, one would think conversing about Jesus would be as natural as talking about the weather. However, at times, I struggle to find the right timing and the right words.

We live in an age that tries to quiet us down by instilling fear about sharing Jesus with those we love. We fear how they will accept it more than we fear what will happen if we do not share our faith. However, after Jesus's resurrection from the dead, He admonished His followers by saying that one of our main duties as believers in Jesus Christ is making disciples. These scriptures are stated more as commands than requests.

> Therefore go and make disciples of all nations, baptizing them in the name of the Father and of the Son and of the Holy Spirit, and teaching them to obey everything I have commanded you. And surely I am with you always, to the very end of the age. (Matthew 28:19–20 NIV)

> But you will receive power when the Holy Spirit comes on you; and you will be my witnesses in

Jerusalem, and in all Judea and Samaria, and to the ends of the earth. (Acts 1:8 NIV)

Just as the disciples shared their faith with each other, we deliberately, over time, share our faith with people we love. In our words and in our actions, we plant seeds and build relationships. Sometimes, however, we worry so much about what to say that we forget we need to be good listeners. God gave us two ears and one mouth for a reason. As we listen to what is important to them, we will begin to see where they are empty and struggling and where there is a void. Then, as God opens doors, we begin to deliberately and delicately share how God can fill the emptiness.

It is often hard to know when to speak up. As you build relationships with people who are not followers of Christ, begin by keeping it simple. Share what God has done in your life. They cannot deny your personal story. Spending time with God in prayer and reading His Word also plays an important role in this. It aids us by making us aware of when God is nudging us to open our mouths. Half the battle is simply opening our mouths and letting God share His love through us. Luke 12:11–12 lets us know we do not need to fret or be afraid about what we will say. The Holy Spirit will give us the words at the right time.

> When you are brought before synagogues, rulers and authorities, do not worry about how you will defend yourselves or what you will say, for the Holy Spirit will teach you at that time what you should say.

There are times when I hesitantly begin to share my faith, and I am amazed at what freely flows out of me. There is no doubt God is speaking through me.

In God's time, as the seeds we planted are watered and fertilized, they will grow and develop. Sometimes, we get discouraged when someone does not accept the Gospel right away. Scripture indicates that we might be the one to plant the seeds, someone else may water them, and God will bring them to fruition in His time. Keep building relationships and planting seeds.

> I planted the seed, Apollos watered it, but God has been making it grow. So neither the one who plants nor the one who waters is anything, but only God, who makes things grow. The one who plants and the one who waters have one purpose, and they will each be rewarded according to their own labor. (1 Corinthians 3:6–8 NIV)

It often takes more time than we want it to take. Keep praying. Keep sharing your faith and living for Jesus in front of the people you love. We also need to pray for boldness as the early church prayed.

> Now, Lord, consider their threats and enable your servants to speak your word with great boldness. (Acts 4:29 NIV)

God, grant us boldness! Make us brave! Like the disciples of Christ, help us share from our hearts what Jesus Christ did on the cross without reservation! The Gospel message is simple. It simply begins with admitting we are sinners, believing in Jesus as our Savior, and confessing our sins. Asking Him to come into our hearts gives us the freedom to live our lives to the fullest. In the midst of serious illness, financial hardship, hurtful relationships, and wherever this journey from birth to death takes us, He came and died so that we could have God-filled, abundant lives.

✎ *Reflection: Regarding your present encounter with Christ, who is God impressing upon you to share your faith with? What is holding you back? Why is it easier to share our latest purchase or home-improvement project than to share our faith about the Savior we love?*

Seaside Name Change
John 1:42

After Andrew shared Jesus with his brother Simon, like so many other times in the scriptures, there was a name change. In this particular incident, Jesus changed Simon's name to Peter. Other examples of name changes in the scriptures include Abram to Abraham (Gen. 17:5), Sarai to Sarah (Gen. 17:15), Jacob to Israel (Gen. 32:28), and Saul to Paul (Acts 13:9).

Changing names was not a new thing. It was an expression of a monumental change in a person's life. Changing Peter's name was not the only difference Jesus made in his life, but it is evident that this newfound faith in Jesus was making him a new person. "Therefore if anyone is in Christ, the new creation has come: the old is gone, the new is here" (2 Corinthians 5:17). A new car soon loses its new car smell. A new outfit is no longer a new outfit after one wear. A new relationship with Jesus Christ, however, can continue to be new as we grow in our faith every day.

> You are a chosen people, a royal priesthood, a holy nation, God's special possession, that you may declare the praises of him who called you out of darkness into his wonderful light. (1 Peter 2:9)

Satan and the world we live in can wear us down and make us forget that we are royalty. Allowing the "newness" to wear off and taking this way of life for granted is easy to do. It is important to remind ourselves of who we belong to and where God has brought us from. We need to remind ourselves that we are children of the King. We possess the resurrecting power of Jesus Christ, which will help us overcome this world and live as He designed us to live. Like Peter, we need to be thankful and celebrate the new name He gave us when we made Him Lord and Savior!

Reflection: When we come to know and believe in Jesus, we take on his name. How has that changed you? What is your new name? Example: Worrier to Warrior? Ruined to Redeemed? What changes do you feel God is trying to make in you—and how would your name change?

Seaside Miracle and Revelation
Luke 5:1-11

Relationships are developed over time. It was no different for the disciples. It was apparent they knew each other. They were fishing buddies, fellow workers, and friends first. Their relationships changed because of a series of seeds that John the Baptist planted and then because of their own personal encounters with Jesus at His baptism. They learned more about Jesus by sitting at His feet and listening to His teachings. Though different in nature and personality, as a tight-knit community of fishermen, they began to have one thing in common: the desire to find and follow the Messiah.

Jesus, because He was God, knew the disciples well. He also had spent enough time with them to know their passion for fishing and what it meant to them on a financial and personal level. On one particular day, Jesus knew the disciples were tired. He knew they had worked all night and had nothing to show for it. He might have also understood that a miracle would seal their faith in Him as the Messiah. Jesus knew their hearts, and He revealed Himself to them in a way that only they would understand: by filling their nets to overflowing. Perhaps it was already their desire, but the miraculous catch of fish precipitated their decision to leave their vocation of fishing and become full-time disciples of Jesus Christ.

Now, to be honest, it would not impress me much if I was fishing and caught more than I needed. I can tell you, however, about a time as a child when I did not have shoes that fit me. My parents could not afford to buy me shoes. I remember humbly kneeling down by my bed one night and praying for shoes. Someone obeyed God and anonymously mailed ten dollars to our home with a note that the money was specifically to be used to buy shoes for Candy. My mom took me to the mall, and I bought four pairs of shoes (two dollars each) and two purses (one dollar each) because of the sales going on. Ha! God knows me. He filled my net overflowing with shoes. New shoes have always been my love language, and Jesus knew how to reveal His love for me and build my faith in Him.

The interesting thing I have seen over time is that God, in His great mercy, knows exactly what will confirm that Jesus is God and how much He cares about us. He knows about those with whom we are sharing our faith, what will speak to them the most, and how to show them that He is real. The little revelations along the way reveal Him as God to them.

✑ *Reflection: How has Jesus made Himself real to you? Who are you closest to who doesn't have a thriving relationship with Jesus? Have you asked Jesus to make Himself real to them?*

Seaside Conviction
Luke 5:8

After getting the miraculous catch of the day, Simon Peter received a revelation that Jesus was the Messiah he had been searching for. He was convicted of his sins, and the holiness of God exposed his sinful nature. Falling down before Jesus, he begged Him to go away from him because he was a sinful man. There is nothing like being in the presence of a holy God to reveal the sin within us.

Likewise, when we are truly living holy lives for God, unsaved people may seem uncomfortable around us. When they see the light of God in us, their dark sinfulness is revealed. It is not us; the holiness of God is convicting them.

For me, it is often an awkward apology for swearing in front of me. Though I have never asked them not to swear in front of me, they know I do not cuss. They know I am a Christian. It is never my intention to make someone feel uncomfortable, but I am thankful they perceive Christ in me. I hope and pray they will desire to know my Savior, Jesus Christ, because of what they see in me.

> For we are to God the pleasing aroma of Christ among those who are being saved and those who are perishing. To the one we are an aroma that brings death; to the other, an aroma that brings life. (2 Corinthians 2:15, 16a)

In other words, to the one who is coming to the knowledge of Jesus Christ, we are the sweet smell of fragrance. To those who are not, we are an unpleasing odor. Smells have a way of filling the air and cannot be ignored. A pumpkin spice candle or an overflowing kitchen wastebasket fills your senses, but both bring different reactions. Likewise, the aroma of the presence of God cannot be ignored.

We never know how people are going to respond to the Holy Spirit in us. We cannot be responsible for their responses. We are only responsible for being a light in a dark world. To some, our faith is received with disgust. To some, we bring the life they desire. Being like Jesus is our greatest responsibility. Some will reject, but others, like Peter, will acknowledge their sins and find life in Jesus Christ.

🖎 *Reflection: Can you think of a time when someone saw the light of Jesus in you, realized you were someone who lives a holy life, and felt uncomfortable around you to the point of conviction? How did you respond?*

Seaside Calling
Luke 5:1–11

While the disciples had already met Jesus and had several encounters with Him, their calling to be full-time disciples did not happen right away, which I had once thought. They were followers, but they had not yet left their regular employment to follow Jesus.

In review of what we have been studying in Luke 5:1–11, Jesus met up with the disciples on the shore. He changed Simon's name, and they experienced a miraculous catch of the day. Peter realized his sin, and then Jesus called James and John, the sons of Zebedee, and Simon into full-time ministry. All of that happened after a long night of fishing beside the Lake of Gennesaret. (The Lake of Gennesaret is also referred to as the Sea of Galilee in other versions of the Bible, as well as by other biblical scholars, like my own father.)

The order in which the disciples were called is uncertain, but this particular story, by the Sea of Galilee, is one of the most read and talked about in sermons. Jesus met them on the job, at the seashore, in their regular vocation of fishing. It was in this setting that He called Simon, James, and John to be His disciples. They had a vocation change. They were no longer fishermen. They were called to be fishers of men.

It is important to take note that Jesus spoke not only to the disciples but to the people all around Him, right where they lived and worked—on the shore. He did not invite them to the synagogue so He could preach to them. Our church buildings are nice places to invite people, but our ministry cannot be limited to places of worship. Instead, in our daily interactions—in grocery stores, in restaurants, in workplaces, and wherever else people are present—we need to have our spiritual antennae up to recognize opportunities to share our faith. Jesus, very naturally and comfortably, sat in a boat and began to teach anyone who was willing to listen. Likewise, Jesus is calling out to people around us and using us to speak the truth to them.

📝 Reflection: Write down some examples of places you have been outside the church where God used you to share your faith. How can you be more aware of who the Holy Spirit is asking you to speak to about Him—and how can you prepare for these encounters?

Seaside Sacrifice
Luke 5:11

Last but not least, the disciples' belief in Jesus as the Messiah caused them to leave everything behind to follow Jesus. Our love for Him must be greater than our love for the things of this world. I am afraid we are often guilty of giving more attention to our daily lives than to our eternal lives. Following Jesus requires a willing sacrifice:

> Then he called the crowd to him along with His disciples and said: "Whoever wants to be my disciple must deny themselves and take up their cross and follow me. For whoever wants to save their life will lose it, but whoever loses their life for me and for the Gospel will save it. What good is it for someone to gain the whole world, yet forfeit their soul? Or what can anyone give in exchange for their soul? If anyone is ashamed of me and my words in this adulterous and sinful generation, the Son of Man will be ashamed of them when he comes in his Father's glory with the holy angels." (Mark 8:34–38 NIV)

In America, we know little about persecution—at least not like our brothers and sisters in Christ across the sea. Americans are busy and often lax in reading our Bibles and maintaining our relationships with God. Making it a priority to come to midweek Bible study is difficult. Vacations no longer include visiting churches while away. We tend to believe whatever we are told, and we have yet to study the Bible for ourselves. Most, when questioned, know little about what they believe.

Only being fed spiritually on Sunday mornings, parishioners jump from church to church because they were not being fed by their previous pastors. It appears that we are more interested in what works and what is comfortable. Satan loves seeing us busy all the time, crowding out time for God. If persecution were to come our way, I am not sure we would have the passion for Christ that would cause us to be willing to die for the cause of Christ. With the emphasis on "me," we cannot live out Mark 8:34–38. God, help us put You first in all our daily activities!

James Elliot (October 8, 1927–January 8, 1956)[3] was an evangelical Christian who was one of five missionaries killed while participating in Operation Auca,[4] an attempt to evangelize the Huaorani people of Ecuador. He is known for saying, "He is no fool who gives what he cannot keep to gain what he cannot lose." Jim Elliot died at the hand of the Aucas, never seeing what his faith envisioned. His selfless life, however, was not in vain. His wife and son stayed and became instrumental in helping the Aucas come to the saving knowledge of Jesus Christ. Jim Elliot, like the disciples, gave all in following Christ.

Following Christ might not require losing one's life for the sake of the Gospel, but according to God's Word, it does require denying self and surrendering to God. Jesus gave His all for us. Like the disciples, we need to be willing to give all to Him.

Reflection: What sacrifices are you making and is God impressing upon you to make for the sake of the Gospel?

---

[3] Wikipedia, s.v. "Jim Elliot," last modified May 31 2019, 18:50, https://en.wikipedia.org/wiki/Jim_Elliot.

[4] "Jim Elliot: Story and Legacy," *Christianity.com*, July 16, 2010 https://www.christianity.com/church/church-history/timeline/1-300/jim-elliot-no-fool-11634862.html.

Conclusion

Matthew was called to be a disciple in Matthew 9:9, but it is biblically unclear what order the remaining disciples were called by Jesus. Throughout the scriptures, however, we see their stories of how God used them for the kingdom's sake.

There are no stereotypes to determine who God calls. The disciples were so different from each other, and so are we. Avoid the comparison trap and allow God to use you right where you are in the way He created you to be. We cannot become cookie-cutter followers of Christ and be effective in ministry. God needs all of us and our quirky personalities, experiences, gifts, talents, failures, successes, hurts, and fears—all of it—to further His kingdom. God is calling you to be His disciple. Jump in with both feet and treasure the journey.

> These are the names of the twelve apostles: first, Simon (who is called Peter) and his brother Andrew; James son of Zebedee, and his brother John; Philip and Bartholomew; Thomas and Matthew the tax collector; James son of Alphaeus, and Thaddaeus; Simon the Zealot and Judas Iscariot, who betrayed him. (Matthew 10:2–4 NIV)

Reflection: What's your story—and how did God call you?

LESSON 3
The Woman at the Well
Scripture References: John 4

The story of the Samaritan woman by the well did not take place near an ocean, a river, a pond, or a sea, but she was standing near water when she met Jesus. As a woman, I cannot pass this story by. Before we delve into the story, be sure to read John 4 in its entirety to see the whole picture of what took place in this story. Then, as we proceed through the lesson, we will refer back to the verses in each section that apply.

Samaritans and Women
John 4:1-6

In verse 1, we read that the Pharisees were unhappy because Jesus was getting some recognition among the people because of His teachings and miracles. Jesus got wind of it and decided to go back to Galilee. In doing so, He went through Samaria. Going through Samaria may not seem like a big deal unless you know the history of Samaria and how much the Jews disliked the Samaritans.

The history of Samaria is written in 2 Kings 17. In this chapter, we learn that because the children of Israel were disobedient and practiced idolatry, God allowed Samaria to be taken captive by the king of Assyria. During their captivity and exile, the king of Assyria brought people from other nations into Samaria. Very simply, they mixed the religion of the Israelites and the religions of the other countries. This was clearly not the desire of God, and He spoke very clearly that they were not to worship any other gods (Exodus 20:1-6). They also began to intermarry and were known as "half-breeds"—mutts, so to speak. They were not pure-blooded Jews. Thus, they were not accepted by the Jews.

At a well in Samaria, Jesus met an unnamed Samaritan woman. She already had two strikes against her—she was a Samaritan, and she was a woman—but Jesus seemed to pay no mind to either of these.

One of the changes that has taken place in history is how women are regarded. To understand why this story is so significant, we must understand the differences in how women were treated in the Old Testament versus the environment in which Jesus was living. In researching this, I discovered an article from a newsletter posted on the Jews for Jesus website regarding "Jesus and the Role of Women," which Zhava Glaser wrote. Glaser says:

> Jesus was a revolutionary. His actions elicited surprising reactions from his contemporaries in all

facets of life. He was not afraid to challenge the status quo and reestablish Scriptural precedents. But without a knowledge of the rabbinic attitudes that prevailed in Jesus' day, the uniqueness of our Lord's behavior escapes us.

Take, for example, Jesus' dealings with women. By publicly including women in his ministry, Jesus shattered the prejudicial customs of his day. Why was it unusual for Jesus to speak with women? Nothing in the Mosaic Law prevented men and women from conversing with one another! Yet the society of Jesus' day, with custom dictated by rabbinic Judaism, differed strikingly from the Old Testament social order.

Women were held in high regard in Old Testament times

The social condition of women in the first century had been radically altered from that of their Old Testament sisters. In earlier times women participated in every aspect of community life except the Temple priesthood. Women freely engaged in commerce and real estate (Prov. 31), as well as in manual labor (Ex. 35:25; Ruth 2:7; 1 Sam. 8:13). They were not excluded from Temple worship. Women played music in the sanctuary (Ps. 68:25), prayed there (1 Sam 1:12), sang and danced with men in religious processions (2 Sam 6:19, 22) and participated in music and festivities at weddings (Song of Songs 2:7, 3:11).

Women were included when God instituted the Mosaic covenant (Deut. 29:11), and were present when Joshua read the Torah to Israel.

Their presence was not just an option; they were required to be present for the public reading of the Scriptures on the Feast of Tabernacles (Deut. 31:12).

Nor were women limited to private roles back then. Several exercised leadership roles over Israel. Miriam led the women of Israel in worship (Ex. 15:20–21); Deborah was a judge and a prophetess (Judges 4:4); and Huldah also was a prophetess, whom King Josiah consulted instead of Jeremiah, her contemporary (2 Kings 22:14–20).

Women were held in high regard in Old Testament times. In Gen. 21:12 we read that God told Abraham to listen to his wife. Proverbs 18:22 tells us that he who finds a wife finds a good thing and Proverbs 19:14 says that an intelligent wife is a gift from God. Wise women also found their way into the pages of the Bible: Abigail's wisdom and valor so touched King David that she became his wife (1 Sam. 25:23–42); and the wise woman of Tekoa was sent to persuade David to lift the ban on his son Absalom (2 Sam. 14).

By New Testament times, women's rights had declined.

By the time of Christ, however, the role of women had drastically changed for the worse. In theory, women were held in high regard by first-century Jewish society, but in practice, this was not always true. The concept of *tzenuah*, or the private role of the woman, was based on Psalm 45:13: The king's daughter is all glorious within. ..." While a man's primary responsibility was seen as public, a woman's life was confined almost entirely within the private family sphere.

Women were not allowed to testify in court. In effect, this categorized them with Gentiles, minors, deaf-mutes and "undesirables" such as gamblers, the insane, usurers, and pigeon-racers, who were also denied that privilege. (On the other hand, a king could not bear witness in court, nor could the Messiah, which somewhat lessens the stigma of that restriction.)

Customarily, even a woman of stature could not engage in commerce and would rarely be seen outside her home. Only a woman in dire economic straits, who was forced to become the family breadwinner, could engage in her own small trade. If a woman was ever in the streets, she was to be heavily veiled and was prohibited from conversing with men. "It is the way of a woman to stay at home and it is the way of a man to go out into the marketplace" (Bereshit Rabbah 18:1; cf. Taanit 23b).

In Talmudic times, respectable women were expected to stay within the confines of the home. The terminology for a prostitute was "one who goes abroad." The woman of the first century did not even do her own shopping, except possibly to go out, accompanied by a slave, to buy material which she would use to construct her own clothing at home!

The women with whom Jesus spoke were very likely illiterate, since the rabbis did not consider it incumbent upon women to learn to read in order to study the Scriptures. Based on the passage in Deut. 4:9, "teach them to thy sons," the rabbis declared women to be exempt from the commandment to learn the Law of Moses. Indeed, the Talmud says, "It is foolishness to teach Torah to your daughter" (Sotah 20a).

Women were separated from men in private, public and religious life. They could go to the Temple, but could not venture beyond the confines of the Women's Court (there was no such court found in the Biblical descriptions of Solomon's Temple). Women were not allowed to participate in public prayer at the Temple, although they were encouraged to have private prayer lives at home.

The few rights of a woman included her right to go to the House of Study to hear a sermon or pray (Vayikra Rabbah, Sotah 22a). Also, it was her basic right to attend a wedding feast or a house of mourning, or to visit her relatives (Mishnah Ketubot 7:5).

One Talmudic passage perhaps best sums up the situation of women at the time of Christ: "(They are) swathed like a mourner (referring to the face and hair coverings) isolated from people and shut up in prison" (Eruvin 100b).

What brought about this drastic change from the esteem women had in Biblical times to their near exclusion from society by the first century? Very likely this degraded view of a woman's role was imported from Greek thought. The similarities between the Hellenistic and Talmudic views of women are remarkable! Through the influence of their heathen neighbors the rabbis slowly relegated women to their first-century seclusion.

Jesus was a revolutionary in his regard for women.

Jesus shattered this darkness by offering his teachings freely to anyone who would listen—whether they were women or men! We see him directly talking with women on numerous occasions. The woman at the well is perhaps the best known of these. We sense the astounded reactions of the disciples that their teacher should be seen talking with a woman. They "marvelled that he talked with the woman. Yet no man said, 'What seekest thou?' or, 'Why talkest thou with her?'" (John 4:27)

In Luke, we see Jesus publicly associating with women. Some were women of high standing in society, some were women of ill repute; and some even had been possessed by demons. One of these—Mary Magdalene, who in great thankfulness was with him until the moment he died—was the first person to whom he appeared after his resurrection.

In Matthew 15:22–28, Jesus spoke with a Canaanite woman. The disciples urged him to send her away, for it was improper for a teacher to speak with a woman, and a foreign one at that! At first, Jesus did not answer her plea for help. But, as she prevailed upon him with her great need and even greater faith, he had mercy on her and granted her request.

Time after time in the Gospels, we see Jesus offering his teachings, healing and forgiveness to women as well as men. Often it was the women who were the most appreciative of his ministry. Indeed, the first proclaimer of Jesus to the Jewish people was a woman—Anna in the Temple (Lk.

2:36–38). A woman washed the Savior's feet (Lk. 7:37–38) and anointed him for his burial (Mk. 14:3). It was women who were with him at the cross until the end (Mk. 15:47), and women who were the first to come to the tomb (Jn. 20:1) and proclaim his resurrection (Mt. 28:8).

Jesus' New Testament followers continued to follow in his footsteps, including women in their gatherings (Acts 1:14) and counting them as co-laborers for Christ (Rom. 16:3). This was only fitting, for Jesus the Messiah, in his love, shattered the restricted status of women in the rabbinic times in which he lived. Because of him, *all* individuals, Jew or Greek, slave or free, *male or female*, can be one in Christ and enjoy unequalled freedom as children of God! [5]

By understanding what a Samaritan was and the way women were regarded, we can better understand the environment Jesus was in when He talked with the Samaritan woman at the well.

✎ *Reflection: What did you learn about in regard to how Jesus wants women to be viewed? How is that different from the way today's world treats women? How does this change your perspective?*

---

[5] Zhava Glaser, "Jesus and the Role of Women," *Jews for Jesus*, June 1, 1988, https://jewsforjesus.org/publications/newsletter/newsletter-jun-1988/jesus-and-the-role-of-women/.

Well-Side Meeting and Conversation
John 4:7–18

First of all, Jesus was tired and thirsty after a long day of travel. The sixth hour in Roman time was around noon. The disciples went to get food. No one was there except for the Samaritan woman who had come to draw water. The fact that she went alone in the hottest part of the day raises a red flag, but we soon find out more. This was not by accident. It was a divine appointment.

Jesus asked her for water.

She said, "You are a Jew, and I am a Samaritan woman. How can you ask me for a drink?"

Jesus replied, "If you knew who I was, you would ask me for a drink."

She asked, "You do not even have anything to draw water with, and this is a deep well. Are you better than Jacob, the one who dug this well for us?"

Then the thirst-quencher's response: "Everyone who drinks this water will be thirsty again, but whoever drinks the water I give him will never thirst. Indeed, the water I give him will become in him a spring of water welling up to eternal life."

Of course, she wanted the water Jesus spoke of so she would never be thirsty again and would never have to go back to the well!

Jesus threw a clincher—and got to the bottom of her spiritual condition. Jesus asked her to go get her husband and come back.

She responded, "I have no husband."

Jesus said, "That's true. You have had five husbands and are now living with someone to whom you are not married."

This explains why she came at noon when no one else was around. She was not exactly esteemed by her community or her female comrades for her moral lifestyle.

Jesus did not shun her as others did. He met her right where she was. He reached out to her in love "just the way she was." He did not expect her to get it all together first. He saw past the hurt to her heart.

As women, we often put such high standards on ourselves. Trying to get it all together, we are harder on ourselves than we are on anyone else. We put on a façade, but we are often living with guilt, self-condemnation, and worry. Jesus is reaching out to us and offering to give us living water through Him without condemnation (Romans 8:1).

Reflection: Do you believe Jesus loves you? Do you believe He wants to speak changes into your life that will give you respect and honor with God—even when they don't come from those who know you and hang on to the old you?

Well-Side Conversions
John 4:19–26, 29, 39–42

After Jesus reveals her spiritual condition, the woman at the well sidesteps the conversation, changes the conversation, and asks a question that was no doubt troubling her regarding where to worship. When you keep in mind that this was being asked by a Samaritan, you understand why this was important to her. Being excluded from Jewish worship, her inward desire to please God was squelched due to the history of her ancestors. And so, seemingly out of nowhere, this deep-seated question arises, but God knew her heart and that this was a real concern for her.

Jesus did not disregard her question. He was not condescending. He answered her and revealed Himself to her. She immediately left behind her water jar and ran off to tell her people. Because of her enthusiasm and joy, they left what they were in the middle of doing and made their way to Jesus. Because of the change in her, they were curious and took a lunch break. No matter what they had to do—and no matter the inconvenience—they went to the well to see Jesus for themselves.

I wonder if our testimony is that convincing. I wonder if the changes in us make people want to seek out Jesus. The Bible tells us that when the people came to Jesus, they believed. Why? Because of her testimony.

Your testimony is the most important thing you have. It is your story of what you were like before you knew Jesus, how you came to know Jesus, and how your life has changed because of Him. No one can argue with your personal story.

Refection: Write out your story.
Before Christ ...
During my conversion ...
Since Christ ...

Well-Side Teaching
John 4:27–38

While the woman at the well was conversing with Jesus, the disciples returned from getting food. When they saw Jesus speaking to her, they had a little meltdown and questioned why He was talking to her. In that culture, one can understand why they were concerned about Jesus talking to a Samaritan woman. After all, she was a Samaritan, *and* she was a woman.

Jesus, as He often did, used this time as a teaching tool to explain to them that there are more important things than eating or drinking, like planting seeds of truth and reaping a harvest.

I cannot be too harsh on the disciples for their insensitivity to what had just happened with Jesus and the woman at the well. I am often disturbed by my lack of concern about the lost, my judgmental attitude toward people, my self-righteousness, and even my discrimination. Like the disciples, I am blinded to the real needs around me. I even lack in faith for their redemption and restoration. Despite my lack of faith, I have seen the worst of sinners redeemed and marriages that seemed unfixable restored. God specializes in the impossible.

In verses 35–38, He uses the metaphor of the harvest:

> The harvest is plentiful, but the workers are few.
> Ask the Lord of the harvest, therefore, to send out
> workers into His fields.

Harvesting is not a one-man job. In northeast Ohio, nurseries hire many men and women for harvesting during the summer months. Likewise, God is "hiring" anyone who is ready and willing to be His servant/employee. The kingdom cannot be advanced if we leave it all up to the Billy Grahams of the world. By doing our own parts to live redeemed lifestyles around those with whom we rub shoulders, each of us can make a difference in leading others to desire and know Jesus as their personal Lord and Savior.

🖎 *Reflection: Who are you writing off as someone who will never come to know Christ? Who do you have prejudices against and hold back from sharing what God has done in your life?*

We have to remember that we were all the woman at the well before we knew Christ. We need to ask the Holy Spirit to help us have a keen sense of His leading to speak to people about Christ. God delivered some of us from lives of bondage, and our testimonies come with amazing stories about God's changes in our lives. God's keeping power kept others of us from lives of bondage. It is growing us and making us the people we would not be without Him. The same power of God that saves is the same power of God that keeps. We may not have a woman at the well story to share, but we all have ways that God has changed us and continues to change us.

Jesus reached out to the woman at the well—a person who was disregarded in her society—and this divine appointment totally changed her life. Today may be that day for you.

Jesus is still asking, "Is anyone thirsty for the water that only I can give?"

This water cleans, purifies, heals, gives life, and satisfies our souls. The good news is that it does not have to be a onetime occurrence. We can drink daily from the well of life by spending time in His Word, praying, and becoming a part of the bigger picture of God's harvest.

LESSON 4
The Parables
Scripture References: Matthew 13:1–52

In Matthew 13, Jesus went out of the house, sat by the lake, and began to speak to the people in parables. What are parables? According to the dictionary,[6] a parable is a short allegorical story designed to illustrate or teach some truth, religious principle, or moral lesson. Stories also help us remember a message long after it has been preached. No doubt, the most interesting speakers are those who use stories to illustrate their points.

---

[6] Dictionary.com, s.v. "parable," http://www.dictionary.com/browse/parable?s=t.

Parable 1 by the Lake
Matthew 13:1–23

In chapter 13, there are several parables. The first one is the parable of the sower. In this parable, Jesus was talking to them in terms they could understand. He was talking about their livelihood. Living near water, they no doubt were farmers by trade. Those who were farmers understood the importance of the soil.

In northeast Ohio, by Lake Erie, the soil is rich due to the glaciers that moved through, leaving sediments that are conducive for vineyards and nurseries. In fact, northeast Ohio was once the rose capital of the nation until the land was sold and began to be built up with houses and businesses. Because I am not one who works in the vineyards or the nurseries, I did not really understand the value of the soil until I ran across this information[7] regarding soil in Ohio.

> Soil scientist have identified more than 400 different types of soil in Ohio, varying according to composition (proportion of sand, silt and clay particles), structure, thickness of layers and dept to bedrock, fertility, pH, drainage, slope and other factors. The differences can matter a lot. The particular soil under your feet can determine what you can grow, whether you can sensibly build a house, or whether a septic system should or should not be installed. Your local soils may even affect your nutrition if you eat locally grown foods or boost your immune system if you inhale or ingest certain soil-borne bacteria.

---

[7] "Soils of a verdant land," Green City Blue Lake: The Cleveland Museum of Natural History, http://www.gcbl.org/explore/land/soils.

Jesus's lesson is simple. There are four different soils and four different outcomes. The *along-the-path* soil is ground that has been hardened by people walking over it repeatedly; the seed remains on top, and the birds come along to eat it. The *rocky soil* is shallow with little soil; plants cannot take root or withstand the sun, and they wither and die. In the *thorny soil*, plants grow up among the thorns; the thorny weeds take over and choke out the good plants. The *good soil* is fertile ground for growth.

The disciples ask, "Why do you speak to us in these stories?"

Jesus gave them his purpose for the parables, and He quoted an Old Testament scripture any studiers of the Law would have known (Isaiah 6:9–10). Jesus continued and did not leave the disciples—or us—clueless about what He was implying. He applied a spiritual principle to the four different soils (of the heart) and the four different responses (of the heart).

In regard to the along-the-path soil, like the birds, the evil one comes and snatches away what has been sown in the heart. The seed never has an opportunity to take root. A person with rocky soil receives Jesus with joy. They seem to grow fast, but because they never allow Jesus to really de-stone them, it's a shallow relationship. Then life happens, and you never see them again. The person with thorny soil hears about Jesus and His Word but is too caught up in this life. Things of no eternal value crowd out what matters most. The good soil represents someone who hears the Word, understands it, and purposefully does what they can to live a godly, Spirit-filled, holy life that is fruitful.

One must avoid the temptation to label people you know as a certain type of soil. It is easier to determine other people's downfalls than our own. At times, we may feel like we are a little bit of each of these soils. God is at work in our lives when He reveals what type of soil we are. The good news is that we can decide how we receive the seed of God's Word. Just like weeding a garden is work and constant, it is a never-ending battle to work with

God and allow Him to water, fertilize, break up the hard places, de-weed, and de-stone our hearts so that we can be fruitful.

🖎 *Reflection: How would you describe the soil of your heart toward things of God? What do you need to change to make yourself more receptive?*

Parable 2 by the Lake
Matthew 13:24–30, 36–43

Again, this story was spoken to people who were in the agricultural industry. They understood the significance of having weeds that looked like wheat growing up together with the wheat. Easily mistaken for wheat, pulling the weed out ahead of harvest time would risk pulling out the good wheat at the same time, so they left them alone until the harvest.

I am far from a horticulturist, but when I am weeding in the spring, it is not always easy to tell which green sprouts are weeds and which ones are perennials. Sometimes the weeds are so close to the flower that, in my haste to get the job done, I pull both out accidentally. Waiting a week for a little more growth, or even a day, would have allowed me to see the difference between the two.

The scripture says the evil one, Satan, planted the weed. Because he is a deceiver, he plants things that look real but are not. The fakes often look real enough to fool us. From TV evangelists to religious groups that take part of the truth and mix it with their own beliefs, we encounter false teachers who surround the false with enough truth to make it look and sound right.

I, as well as others I know, have received Facebook scams. In one instance, I am embarrassed to say, I was almost fooled until I looked at it more closely. How do con artists convince intelligent people to send money to them? By building a case and appearing real.

We need to study God's Word to know what we believe and to be able to discern what is false. We cannot be naïve and open to every philosophy. If we are actively following Jesus, the prodding of the Holy Spirit should awaken our spiritual antennae and alert us to what is untrue.

Once, someone I loved very deeply was being pursued by a cult. On the surface, the religious organization seemed to be a Christian, Bible-believing organization, but as we bought resources to help us understand their whole doctrinal stance, we soon discovered it was not biblical at all. God used me to help them see where the religious philosophies would take them, and they reconsidered their decision.

On another occasion, our church had a series of studies. I was in the class and sensed that something did not seem right, but it took a while to realize we needed to cancel the class. Again, on the surface, it seemed right, and people in the class were experiencing benefits from the study. As the study proceeded, however, we discovered some of the doctrinal beliefs were unscriptural—and ultimately unhealthy. Even though something has the label "Christian" or quotes scripture, we still need to hold it up to the entire Bible and not accept it unless it is in line with God's Word.

Satan wants to do whatever he can to make us accept the counterfeit. He plants the fake along with the real, hoping we do not notice. Just as bankers study a real dollar bill in order to be able to identify a counterfeit one, we need to study the Bible to know what is real. Staying in connection with people who study the Bible holds us accountable if we start embracing false theology. There are no lone rangers in Christianity. We need each other while praying for spiritual maturity.

Reflection: Have you ever been fooled by something that sounded right but was not correct according to God's Word? How did God reveal the truth to you?

In verses 36–43, we read of the outcome for the counterfeit wheat, which is hell. This picture of a place where there will be weeping and gnashing of teeth is not to be taken lightly. Instead, it should help us embrace a healthy fear and reverence for a loving God who also will one day judge the earth and punish sin. On the other hand, the reward for the righteous, the pure wheat, will be living in the presence of their heavenly Father.

Parable 3 by the Lake
Matthew 13:31–33

The parables of the mustard seed and the yeast are different yet similar. They teach us that something very small—like the mustard seed that grew into a large tree or the yeast used to bake a fresh loaf of bread—can transform into something much larger and more useful for the kingdom.

Jesus came into the world—to the small, obscure town of Bethlehem—to unknown parents. To the religious people of the day, it seemed inconceivable that God would use Jesus, a small-town boy, to be the Savior of the world. Even His disciples, the blue-collar workers of the day, though seen as small in the eyes of the upper class, would be used by God to change history.

Throughout history, God used the unlikely to do His work. He is not impressed with the people who we might choose. We are often influenced by people who are bigger than life—good-looking, wealthy, gifted, charismatic people—but God sees past the façade to the seeds of the heart.

In Mark 9:35, Jesus tells His disciples, "Anyone who wants to be first must be the very last, and the servant of all." My dad taught me long ago to have the heart of a servant if you want to be used by God. He would say, "Don't expect to be the leader of a ministry if you are unwilling to clean toilets." In our small home mission church, we did it all—whatever it took—to make ministry happen on Sunday mornings.

In my thirties, while I was getting ready for a youth event one evening, I was conversing with another youth minister—who since has gone on to be with Jesus—about the work that was involved in doing youth ministry. At times, it seemed to yield little reward. He said something to me that I will never forget: "Anything that is worth doing isn't without a lot of work."

We often put the cart before the horse. There is so much talk about setting ginormous goals and envisioning enormous dreams.

I am not opposed to expressing a vision for the end result, but it seems like we want the end result without all the hard knocks and bruises along the way. We need to be content in our small beginnings, have servants' hearts, and let God decide what large outcomes, if any, will result. His dreams are big for us, yet they are different from what we can imagine.

🖎 *Reflection: Can you think of some biblical or modern-day examples where God used the unlikely in big ways? Consider Samuel. Joseph. Moses. the boy with the small lunch. Saul. etc.*

It takes a small seed to grow a large tree. It takes a little bit of leaven (yeast) to turn wheat into the dough for a loaf of bread. God takes what little we have and multiplies it for His purpose. If you want to be great in God's kingdom, remember your small beginnings and be a servant of all.

Parable 4 by the Lake
Matthew 13:44–46

The two parables in this passage—the parable of the hidden treasure and the parable of the pearl—are very similar. They illustrate Jesus's point that when finding something of great value, one would sacrifice everything else that was once valued to have it.

The treasure and the pearl represent the salvation Jesus gives. We cannot purchase salvation. Salvation was already purchased for us at a "great price" by Jesus. When we realize this, it is no wonder that we count all losses to follow our treasure, Jesus, and the salvation He gives. Apostle Paul, in Philippians 3, wrote about the value of knowing Jesus:

> But whatever were gains to me I now consider loss for the sake of Christ. What is more, I consider everything a loss because of the surpassing worth of knowing Christ Jesus my Lord, for whose sake I have lost all things. I consider them garbage, that I may gain Christ and be found in him, not having a righteousness of my own that comes from the law, but that which is through faith in Christ—the righteousness that comes from God on the basis of faith. (Philippians 3:7–9 NIV)

Paul realized that having the gift of salvation, the presence and blessing of Jesus in His life, was priceless to the point of giving all for this great gift. Having Jesus in our lives becomes more important than health, wealth, fame, and family; anything we consider important pales in comparison to being in a right relationship with Him. Once we find Him, we are spiritually satisfied—and our search is over.

Reflection: Is there anything or anyone in your life who competes with your desire to live for Jesus?

Parable 5 by the Lake
Matthew 13:47–52

When a net is let down into the bottom of a lake or pond to collect fish or game, it collects whatever is presently there. One would think that a fish is a fish, but in this parable, some were not edible; some were even dead or rotten. The good are kept, and the bad are disposed of. Jesus interprets this for the disciples by letting them know that at the end of time, the wicked will be separated from the righteous and sent to a fiery furnace, and there will be weeping and gnashing of teeth. On several occasions throughout the New Testament, Jesus makes a point to let His disciples and followers know that not everyone "in the net" is going to heaven.

Like the net in this parable, the Gospel attracts various types of people. Some are true followers, and others are not. Abraham Lincoln said, "You can fool all the people some of the time, and some of the people all the time, but you cannot fool all the people all the time." Just as going into the garage does not make someone a car, going to church does not guarantee someone will be a Christ follower. It may be hard for us to tell if someone is really living for God, but God knows—and He is not fooled. In the end, He will be the Judge.

It is a very sobering thought about the end of time when people's hearts will be revealed as to whether they truly had relationships with Jesus and were living for Him.

> Many will say to me on that day, "Lord, Lord, did we not prophesy in your name and in your name drive out demons and in your name perform many miracles?" Then I will tell them plainly, "I never knew you. Away from me, you evildoers!" (Matthew 7:22–23 NIV)

Just as there is a difference between knowing about someone and knowing them, there is a difference in knowing of Jesus and truly knowing Him. The good news is this: from the Garden of Eden on, God has desired fellowship with us. He wants to know us, and He wants us to have a relationship with Him. He made a way through Jesus Christ. The good news for us continues: we can be authentic followers of Jesus Christ by carefully studying His Word and applying it to our daily lives. The good news for us goes further: in the book of Acts, chapter 1, when Jesus left the earth, He did not leave us without the sanctifying power of the Holy Spirit, which helps us live sinless lives. Now is the time.

✎ *Reflection: Personally, looking into your heart, what is God pointing out to you that needs to change to be an authentic follower of Jesus Christ?*

LESSON 5
In the Storm
Scripture Reference: Matthew 14

At the start of chapter 14 in the book of Matthew, John the Baptist has been beheaded. The disciples buried the body of John and went to tell Jesus. When Jesus received this news, He dismissed Himself from their presence and the activities around Him. Experiencing His own personal storm, He found a private place to be alone, possibly to mourn.

A Quiet Place in the Storm
Matthew 14:22, 23

Sometimes life happens, and we find ourselves wanting things to stop. We find ourselves needing to get away from the demands of life to deal with the present storms in our lives. Jesus was no different. Public ministry had left Him with little privacy. Throughout the Gospels, there are several mentions of Jesus getting alone in prayer, by Himself, to gain comfort and strength, to pray, and to seek God's will. If Jesus, being fully God and fully man, needed time to mourn and gain comfort, we also have times when we need to be alone with God.

Before the storm, in the middle of the storm, or after the storm, circumstances can drive us to our knees, out of sight, alone with God. On some days, we need it more than others; even so, those places and times of gathering ourselves in thought and prayer seem hard to find, are short-lived, or are abruptly interrupted.

Young moms especially have a hard time getting away from it all. On duty 24/7, hoping no one will notice, they sneak into the bathroom because it is the only place to get away where no one will bother them. Then, their silent moment of refuge is quickly broken when their children knock on the door. "Mom? Mom! What are you doing? I need you!" Just like our children find us, just like the schedule awaits us when we walk out of our quiet place, Jesus was bombarded by a crowd of people, which resulted in a day of ministry and the miracle of feeding five thousand people with a lunch that was meant for one.

Just like Jesus, we need to shut out the noise and be still with our heavenly Father. With all the demands of life on us—work, family, home, and ministries within the community and church— this is hard to do. Quiet time is important for your physical health, mental health, emotional health, and spiritual health.

He says, "Be still, and know that I am God; I will be exalted among the nations, I will be exalted in the earth." (Psalm 46:10 NIV)

Reflection: Do you have a quiet place? A place to be still before God?

God Sees Us in the Storm
Matthew 14:22–24

After another day of hectic ministry, Jesus dismissed the crowd, put the kids to bed, so to speak, sent the disciples out on the boat with instructions to meet Him on the other side, and went up into the mountain to be alone in prayer.

Living by Lake Erie, we have come to know that the lake can be fickle. We enjoy the beauty of the sunsets over the lake, but we also know the perils of the lake. The lake can be calm and look like glass or be rough and treacherous. Because it is a shallow lake, storms can come quickly and be perilous. Many a life has been claimed on Lake Erie due to the strong undertow and unpredictable storms. The Lighthouse Museum in Fairport has displays of many accounts of the Coast Guard's heroic rescue missions and the lives affected by them. Unbeknownst to them, the disciples were about to encounter a frightening storm.

A storm can come in the middle of the night. Storms have a way of sneaking up on us. One moment, you are on a simple boat ride across the lake and then—boom!—out of nowhere, you're in a storm, fighting to make it out alive. If people knew what was ahead, they could prepare or avoid certain situations altogether. Some storms are unavoidable. In the account of this story found in the Gospel of Mark, Jesus sees them struggling in the storm:

> Later that night, the boat was in the middle of the lake, and he was alone on land. He saw the disciples straining at the oars, because the wind was against them. Shortly before dawn he went out to them, walking on the lake. (Mark 6:47–48 NIV)

This scripture encourages me. It reminds me that God always sees what we are going through. The Old Testament story of Hagar is found in Genesis 16. Hagar, a slave of Abram's wife, Sarah, was given to Abram to bear a son since Sarah could not. This was a common practice in that day. Once she was pregnant, Hagar was full of anger and acted out toward Sarah. Sarah was unhappy with Hagar and sent her out to fend on her own.

Hagar was distraught and alone in the desert. An angel appeared, instructed her to go back and submit to Sarah, and gave her a promise about the son she is carrying. Hagar named the Lord, "El Roi, the God who sees me."

> She gave this name to the LORD who spoke to her: "You are the God who sees me," for she said, "I have now seen the One who sees me." That is why the well was called Beer Lahai Roi; it is still there, between Kadesh and Bered. (Genesis 16:13, 14 NIV)

Like Hagar, we may find ourselves in a place in which we are emotionally distraught about our circumstances. The situation may be caused by our environments or by our actions. We can be comforted by knowing that God is the God who sees. He is not blind to what is going on in our lives. God sees the single mom struggling to make ends meet. God sees the family dealing with a recent life-threatening diagnosis of cancer. God sees the marriage struggling to survive. God sees the individual dealing with uncertainties in their career. God sees the injustices and those who are being taken advantage of by others. God sees the parents mourning the loss of an adult child after a heroin overdose. God sees us when we are on the hamster wheel of life and cannot seem to get off. God sees. He knows. He cares.

Reflection: Think about something you are going through right now and the things that led up to bringing you to this place. Can you take comfort in knowing God sees?

God Comes to Us in the Storm
Matthew 14:25–31

In the middle of the darkness of night, Jesus saw the storm the disciples were facing and walked toward them on the water. They were scared to death and thought they were seeing a ghost. They cried out in fear. We cannot be too critical of them being so fearful since fear is often the driving force of the storms we face. We also cannot be too critical of them for not recognizing Jesus. We cannot be critical of Peter for asking Jesus to identify Himself again. How many times have we asked for clarification? We ask God, "If it is really you leading us, please confirm it one more time."

At Jesus's invitation, Peter jumped out of the boat and started walking on the water toward Jesus. It was a step of faith, something he had never done before, but he felt in the moment that he could do anything with Jesus nearby. But like all of us, reality set in, fear took over, he began to sink, and he cried out to God for help! Crying out to God was the right response to the incredibly fearful place he was in.

Hearing Peter's cries, Jesus did not write him off as a failure and let him drown in his ambition. He immediately reached down, and they walked together back to safety. There are times for all of us when we feel like we are drowning in the midst of trying to do something we believe is right. In the middle of the storm, we can reach up and call out to Him. In the middle of the storm, He tells us we can have more faith—and we need not doubt. He stays by our side and guides us to safety. He walks with us in the storm as well as in the calm parts of life.

In Luke 8:22–25, a storm arrived while the disciples were in a boat. Jesus was sound asleep in the bottom of the boat. The disciples cried out to Him for help, and Jesus replied, "You of little faith, why are you so afraid?" He calmed the storm, and the wind and waves subsided. The disciples were amazed. Times like that with Jesus were faith-building moments. Because of times like that, they were better equipped to face the future tsunamis of life because they had experienced the storm and knew Jesus was in control.

Having experienced different types of storms in life, I am never really sure we can ever be completely prepared. However, when people learn to lean on Jesus, letting Him carry them through to safety, it builds a deeper trust and faith in God. There is calmness, an assurance that God has it under control, and a trust that whatever the outcome, He will be there to the bitter end. If everything were simple and easy, we would never develop confidence in God that He is with us in the storm.

Matthew 14:32 says, "And when they climbed into the boat, the wind died down." It is important to note that Peter's storm did not calm down right away. When Jesus came to his side, there was not immediate tranquility. Jesus continued to walk through the storm with Peter. Once they were in the boat, the wind ceased.

When I cry out to Jesus for help with difficulties of life, I desire instant resolution, but more often than not, I experience what Peter did: a step-by-step, side-by-side stride to completion. Whether a sprint or a marathon, I would rather walk through a storm with Jesus by my side than by myself, alone. The peace that comes from having His presence through the trials of life is invaluable.

Romans 5:3b–5 tells us more benefits of suffering and trials:

> We also glory in our sufferings, because we know that suffering produces perseverance; perseverance, character; and character, hope. And hope does not put us to shame, because God's love has been poured out into our hearts through the Holy Spirit, who has been given to us. (Romans 5:3b–5 NIV)

The growth that comes from trials cannot be gained in any other way. The way we respond to the storms of life defines who we are and who we will become. It is our story. Our testimony. In the difficulties of life, we decide whether to become unusable, hardened clay or moldable, pliable clay, becoming the image of Christ.

Another outcome of the tornados of life is that our experiences can be used to encourage and comfort others who are going through similar circumstances. Paul tells the Corinthians that everything they have endured is not in vain:

> Praise be to the God and Father of our Lord Jesus Christ, the Father of compassion and the God of all comfort, who comforts us in all our troubles, so that we can comfort those in any trouble with the comfort we ourselves receive from God. (2 Corinthians 1:3–4)

Our life experiences can be used to build faith and comfort others when they are going through circumstances that seem unending.

After the storm died down, the disciples realized Jesus was truly God, and they responded with worship. It is not always our second nature to worship. Instead, we tend to worry, be critical, ask questions, and find fault. As a worship leader, it might seem like I have a song for every occasion and have it down pat when it comes to giving God the praise He deserves. Even I can get into the "poor-little-old-me" syndrome and fail to see the opportunity for God to get the glory.

During one particular storm in my life, in which my husband had lost his job and was having difficulty finding a new one, I stopped myself from praying endless prayers about the situation and began to thank God for everything. Half an hour later, I was still giving thanks. I had so many things to be thankful for, and my heavy heart had turned into a thankful heart, knowing that God is a good God and that we would get through this together—just like we had on so many other occasions.

Looking back at how God interceded during other storms in our lives reveals God's goodness and faithfulness to us. This causes us to worship. It builds our faith. Sometimes we walk through storms of life and hold our breath, trying to think through the outcomes and solve them on our own. All Jesus wants us to do is cry out to Him and trust Him. Some storms seem to last forever, but Jesus walks with us. More often than not, we have questions with no answers or solutions during life's stormy situations. Like Peter, we choose to walk with Him and worship Him.

🖎 *Reflection: Recall a situation in which you walked through a storm with Jesus and how that built your faith or a situation that is building your faith now.*

Before closing the book and moving on to the rest of your day or evening, why not spend some time thanking God for the storm you are in and for His past provisions and interventions. Then, begin to pray that God will reveal Himself to someone else you know who is going through a storm. They will see His hand through it and will be able to worship God. Don't let the storm you are going through "go to waste," so to speak. Let it bring God glory in some way.

LESSON 6
By the Sea of Tiberias
Scripture Reference: John 21:1–17

The disciples had just been through an emotional roller coaster: the triumphal entry of Jesus riding on a donkey, the Last Supper, the betrayal, the Crucifixion, and the resurrection. They had just experienced their worst nightmare: seeing their leader whom they loved crucified and laid to rest in a borrowed tomb. They were definitely in need of some R and R.

Though all the disciples fled the scene during the Crucifixion for self-preservation, I feel for Peter the most. He fled—*and* he denied Jesus. Though Jesus predicted he would deny Him three times, the manner in which it played out is most disturbing to me (John 13:31–28; 18:15–18; 25–27).

His first denial was to a servant girl in the high priest's courtyard. Simple enough. What did it matter anyway? He'd never see her again. His second denial was to servants and officials around a campfire. He was simply protecting himself. Again, as if the other two denials had never happened, he denied knowing Jesus a third time to a person related to the one whose ear he had cut off in the Garden of Gethsemane. Immediately, he heard the sound that brought him to his knees: the crow of a rooster. Brokenhearted, he cried like he had never cried before.

All of us have been in similar situations that caught us off guard. Our tongues, hearts, and minds collided in conflict, and our fears overtook what we believe. As we continue with this story, may you see the grace and love that Jesus gave to Peter. It extends to you and me as we learn and grow in our faith journey with Him.

Fellowship by the Sea
John 21:1–3

In John 21—after the Crucifixion and the many confirmed and unconfirmed rumors of Jesus being alive—Peter announced he was going fishing. Dealing with their own loss and sensing Peter's remorse, the disciples did not let Peter go alone.

The disciples had walked many miles together with Jesus. They saw firsthand the miracles, listened to His teachings, and caught glimpses of the heart of God for the world. They were the closest of friends, understood each other's pain, and held each other up in the uncertain circumstances they were facing. They had all been through so much and were all each other had. With all they had been through, they needed to stick together.

Having been in situations where I felt stunned by troubling events and my own nightmares, I found strength in the presence of close friends. Only a close friend would walk with me into an intimidating office situation and help box up my belongings and leave. Only the closest of friends would walk with me, pray, and talk for as long as was needed. Only a friend would help go through the belongings of a deceased mother. Only a friend would sacrifice time—and even money—to help in a crisis. Friends, not acquaintances, know what is best for you. They know how to pray, and they care deeply enough to go the extra mile.

The conversation in the boat that morning must have been like no other. They may have reminisced of days gone by, cried about the recent events, or just sat in silence and stared in disbelief. Perhaps they even wondered what they could have done differently, if anything. Perhaps Peter shared his remorse for denying Jesus. Though the scriptures did not record their dialogue, we can imagine how thankful they were for each other. As they stayed close, they enjoyed doing what they knew how to do best. They relaxed and settled into doing what several of them were doing when Jesus called them to be His disciples—they fished.

We've all heard the saying, "What does fellowship mean? It's two fellows in the same boat." Together, they were in the same boat! There are times when true fellowship helps us get through the various seasons of life we encounter.

Reflection: Describe a time when the closeness and presence of others carried you through a hard time.

Breakfast by the Sea
John 21:4–14

They fished all night, but they caught nothing.

In the morning, unknown to the disciples, Jesus was standing on the beach. Jesus asked the disciples, "Did you catch anything to eat?"

"Nothing," they replied.

Jesus said, "Cast your net on the right side of the boat, and you'll catch some."

So, they cast one more time and caught so much they weren't able to bring it into the boat. That was a dead giveaway.

John said to Peter, "It is the Lord!"

Peter—still belligerent and impulsive in his own way—jumped out of the boat, left the rest to bring the boat and fish ashore, and ran to Jesus.

On the shore, Jesus had built a campfire, and breakfast was already cooking. He invited them to come, bring their catch, and have breakfast with Him.

As a continuation of their fellowship, Jesus offered them food. Though I am not particularly blessed with the gift of hospitality or known for my exquisite cooking skills, I have been the recipient of the hospitality and cooking skills of others and the unity it brought as we ate together. There are many places in the Bible where God made sure His people had food to eat before He ministered to them spiritually.

Elijah was one of those people. In 1 Kings 18, Elijah, in the midst of the prophets of Baal, experienced the great victory of God sending fire down from heaven, consuming the sacrifice, and making Himself known as the one true God. In 1 Kings 19, because of Jezebel threatening to murder him, Elijah found himself discouraged and depressed. He ran into hiding and wished he could die. The first thing God did before addressing the situation or speaking wisdom into Elijah's life was make sure he had nourishment and rest.

In our go-go-go world, God still knows that we need to take time for ourselves. We need proper nourishment and rest. For Peter, it was no different. For us, it is no different.

🖎 *Reflection: Feeling down? Have you been taking care of yourself? Do you know someone who is struggling? How can you help them get some rest and have some healthy nourishment and fellowship?*

Restoration by the Sea
John 21:15–17

No doubt, Peter carried much anguish with him. I would. Wouldn't you? Being human, he had to carry a certain amount of awkward embarrassment, hurt, and anger toward himself for his denials at a time when Jesus needed him the most.

Jesus knew Peter. He knew he needed to get past his regret. He gave him the opportunity to redeem the past and prepare for the future. He asked him three times, "Do you love me?"

The first two times, Peter responded, "Yes, Lord. You know I love you." The third time, hurt that Jesus kept asking him the same question, he said, "Yes, Lord. You know all things. You know that I love you."

As a worship leader, I look out at the congregation during worship, and I am privileged to see the responses of people who shift from merely singing a song to full-out worship in admiration of their Savior who loves them. As people, we come to church carrying the week with us. The worship starts, and our minds are still spinning—and our focus is not where it needs to be. Very seldom are people ready to declare their love for God in full worship on the first note or word. We may be singing, but it is just lyrics. Then, as the worship continues, and we sing through a song or even the whole set, people begin to respond more enthusiastically. There are pat responses, but worship goes beyond the expected. Peter definitely moved from what he was expected to say to a heartfelt response: "Yes, Lord. You know all things. You know that I love you!" Our heartfelt responses to God often signify our intentions.

I do not know if Peter realized that—even though he had denied Jesus three times—he had been given the opportunity to reverse that denial with an affirmation of his love. God, in His great mercy, knew exactly how to help Peter deal with his failures. When praying for people, I often pray, "You made them, God. You know exactly how to get through to them and speak to them in a way they will understand and respond to."

My husband and I have two children. They came from the same parents and were raised in the same household. With one, I could give the mom look; with the other, I had to be stern, raise my voice, and take away privileges to get the desired response. Likewise, some of us respond to a fire-and-brimstone message, and others respond better to message about a tender, loving Savior. Jesus was talking to Peter in a way that only Peter would understand.

Reflection: Can you recall a time when Jesus spoke to you and showed Himself to you in a way you could not deny and brought about the change that was needed in your life?

Change by the Sea
John 21:15–17

Jesus's response was interesting. The first time, Jesus said, "Feed my lambs." The second time, He responded, "Tend my sheep." The last time, He said, "Feed my sheep." The significance of repeating a question three times let Peter know the importance of the answer. Once he was told by Jesus to be a fisher of men; now the tide was changing to feed and tend sheep. Being a shepherd was a definite shift in Peter's ministry.

In Peter 5, Peter instructs the elders of the church to be shepherds of the flock. They were to do more than "catch" or "convert" them. They were to disciple them and care for them as a shepherd cares for his sheep. In 1 Peter 5, Peter's focus was on shepherding—not evangelism:

> To the elders among you, I appeal as a fellow elder and a witness of Christ's sufferings who also will share in the glory to be revealed: Be shepherds of God's flock that is under your care, watching over them—not because you must, but because you are willing, as God wants you to be; not pursuing dishonest gain, but eager to serve; not lording it over those entrusted to you, but being examples to the flock. And when the Chief Shepherd appears, you will receive the crown of glory that will never fade away. (1 Peter 5:1–4 NIV)

Shepherding would require more. It would require caring, watching with pure motives, and a willing servant's heart—not as a dictator but as an example for them to follow, a reflection of our Chief Shepherd.

Throughout the Old and New Testament, there are scriptures that designate God as the Shepherd and God's people as the sheep. Like Peter, one must know the Shepherd before becoming a shepherd.

Psalm 23, one of the most quoted and known, speaks of the Lord as being our Shepherd and the benefits of being his sheep.

> A psalm of David. The LORD is my shepherd, I lack nothing. He makes me lie down in green pastures, he leads me beside quiet waters, he refreshes my soul. He guides me along the right paths for his name's sake. Even though I walk through the darkest valley, I will fear no evil, for you are with me; your rod and your staff, they comfort me. You prepare a table before me in the presence of my enemies. You anoint my head with oil; my cup overflows. Surely your goodness and love will follow me all the days of my life, and I will dwell in the house of the LORD forever. (Psalm 23 NIV)

🖎 *Reflection: When reading Psalm 23. how does this chapter speak to you? How is God being a Shepherd to you currently? How has He been a Shepherd to you in the past?*

John 10 is dedicated to Jesus being our True Shepherd:

> Very truly I tell you Pharisees, anyone who does
> not enter the sheep pen by the gate, but climbs
> in by some other way, is a thief and a robber. The
> one who enters by the gate is the shepherd of the
> sheep. The gatekeeper opens the gate for him, and
> the sheep listen to his voice. He calls his own
> sheep by name and leads them out. When he has
> brought out all his own, he goes on ahead of them,
> and his sheep follow him because they know his
> voice. But they will never follow a stranger; in fact,
> they will run away from him because they do not
> recognize a stranger's voice. (John 10:1–5 NIV)

Jesus continues teaching about the Good Shepherd even though
the Pharisees seemed to have no clue as to what he was trying to
convey to them.

> Therefore Jesus said again, "Very truly I tell you,
> I am the gate for the sheep. All who have come
> before me are thieves and robbers, but the sheep
> have not listened to them. I am the gate; whoever
> enters through me will be saved. They will come
> in and go out, and find pasture. The thief comes
> only to steal and kill and destroy; I have come that
> they may have life, and have it to the full.
>   "I am the good shepherd. The good shepherd
> lays down his life for the sheep. The hired hand is
> not the shepherd and does not own the sheep. So
> when he sees the wolf coming, he abandons the
> sheep and runs away. Then the wolf attacks the
> flock and scatters it. The man runs away because
> he is a hired hand and cares nothing for the sheep.

"I am the good shepherd; I know my sheep and my sheep know me—just as the Father knows me and I know the Father—and I lay down my life for the sheep. I have other sheep that are not of this sheep pen. I must bring them also. They too will listen to my voice, and there shall be one flock and one shepherd. The reason my Father loves me is that I lay down my life—only to take it up again. No one takes it from me, but I lay it down of my own accord. I have authority to lay it down and authority to take it up again. This command I received from my Father." (John 10:7–18 NIV)

John 10 lets us know that Jesus is the True Shepherd. The One who enters by the door and not any other way is the Shepherd. He can be trusted. All others are out to kill, steal, or destroy. The sheep know His voice. The Shepherd knows their names, protects them, and leads them. He goes before them. He would go so far as to lay down His life for His sheep.

In our world today, we have access to the many voices of religious philosophies. We have to be careful to follow the True Shepherd, to study and know His ways so we can recognize His voice. The best way is to get into His Word so you can recognize and discern misleading leaders. Knowing the True Shepherd well will help us be good shepherds to those we are leading.

Peter's experiences with Jesus made him a better shepherd. Our experiences in life, as we grow in Jesus, make us more effective shepherds to those we have a regular influence on. Though we may not be shepherds in the essence that Peter was, we are all shepherding in some way.

Shepherding is not for the faint of heart, and we need to realize that while we may not be pastors or elders of the church, we are all shepherds in one way or another—and people will follow our lead. Whether we are ministry leaders or behind-the-scenes workers, we are leading. We need to emulate the True Shepherd and direct others toward Him and not away from Him.

Our words and actions matter. They can either lead people to Christ or push them away. They can build up or crush down. They can build or divide. We are either positively or negatively affecting the kingdom of God with our leadership. We fool ourselves into thinking we are not affecting the lives of others. We are responsible for the decisions we make and the way we carry ourselves in our churches, workplaces, and, more importantly, our families. That is where our true colors come out and our hearts are revealed.

Reflection: Though you may not always feel like a leader, do you realize you are leading/shepherding? Name an example of this.

One of my favorite references in the Bible regarding sheep is the parable of the lost lamb. This scripture talks about His diligence in looking for us, and it also talks about His joy after finding us.

> Then Jesus told them this parable: "Suppose one of you has a hundred sheep and loses one of them. Doesn't he leave the ninety-nine in the open country and go after the lost sheep until he finds it? And when he finds it, he joyfully puts it on his shoulders and goes home. Then he calls his

friends and neighbors together and says, 'Rejoice with me; I have found my lost sheep.' I tell you that in the same way there will be more rejoicing in heaven over one sinner who repents than over ninety-nine righteous persons who do not need to repent." (Luke 15:3–7 NIV)

Just as Jesus singled out Peter and had a heart-to-heart conversation that restored him and set him on a new path of ministry that influenced the early church, Jesus, in His great mercy and love, hunts us down.

Reflection: Do you realize you are the one sheep that Jesus would leave the flock to go after? Why not spend some time thanking God for coming after you like the lost sheep and praying for those who are on your heart who are not following the True Shepherd?

By the water's edge, Jesus, after being baptized by John the Baptist, called his disciples into full-time ministry. Well-side, He quenched the thirsty soul of the Samaritan woman. On the seashore, He taught spiritual truths through stories to all who would listen. In the middle of the lake, faith-building lessons were learned during a horrific storm. On the shores of Tiberius, Jesus restored Peter to ministry. You may not have an ocean view or a lake front setting, but Jesus is still in the business of calling, healing, teaching, restoring, building, and changing lives. Jesus is a sure way for a weary soul to be refreshed. Like a satisfying cold glass of water on a hot day, He is the Living Water. Like a refreshing vacation with an ocean view, He is the Good Shepherd who leads beside still waters. He is the calm in the storm. He is the God who sees. He is the God who forgives and restores!

Thank you for reading "Encounters with Jesus by the Water." As a new author, I would love to hear your feedback as to how God used this book to speak into your life. Also let me know if you used it as a private devotional or for a group study. To reach out to me, please email me: candyporo@yahoo.com

Printed in the United States
By Bookmasters